About Skill Buil
Readir
Comprehension Grade 4

Welcome to Skill Builders *Reading Comprehension* for fourth grade. This book is designed to improve children's reading comprehension skills through focused practice. The book's eye-catching graphics and engaging topics entice even reluctant readers. Each full-color workbook contains grade-level-appropriate passages and exercises based on national standards to help ensure that children master basic skills before progressing.

More than 70 pages of activities cover essential comprehension strategies, such as inferring, sequencing, and finding the main idea and supporting details. The workbook also contains questions and activities to help children build their vocabularies.

The Skill Builders series offers workbooks that are perfect for keeping skills sharp during the school year or preparing them for the next grade.

Credits:

Content Editors: Ashley Anderson and Elizabeth Swenson
Copy Editor: Julie B. Killian
Layout, Cover Design, and Inside Illustrations: Nick Greenwood

www.carsondellosa.com
Carson-Dellosa Publishing LLC
Greensboro, North Carolina

ISBN 978-1-936023-32-5
04-184121151

Table of Contents

Suggested Reading List

Babbitt, Natalie
Tuck Everlasting

Ballard, Robert D.
Finding the Titanic

Banks, Lynne Reid
The Indian in the Cupboard

Barshaw, Ruth McNally
Ellie McDoodle: Have Pen, Will Travel

Blume, Judy
Tales of a Fourth Grade Nothing; Superfudge

Brink, Carol Ryrie
Caddie Woodlawn

Coville, Bruce
My Teacher Is an Alien

Creech, Sharon
Walk Two Moons

Dahl, Roald
James and the Giant Peach; Charlie and the Chocolate Factory

DiCamillo, Kate
Because of Winn-Dixie

Erickson, John R.
The Original Adventures of Hank the Cowdog

Farber, Erica and Mayer, Mercer
The Alien from Outer Space: A Graphic Novel Adventure

Fitzhugh, Louise
Harriet the Spy

Gardiner, John Reynolds
Stone Fox

Hamilton, Virginia
The House of Dies Drear

Howe, Deborah and James
Bunnicula: A Rabbit-Tale of Mystery

L'Engle, Madeleine
A Wrinkle in Time

Levine, Ellen
Henry's Freedom Box: A True Story from the Underground Railroad

Levine, Gail Carson
Ella Enchanted

Lewis, C. S.
The Lion, the Witch and the Wardrobe

MacLachlan, Patricia
Sarah, Plain and Tall

Martin, Ann M.
A Dog's Life: The Autobiography of a Stray

Nicklin, Flip and Linda
Face to Face with Dolphins

O'Dell, Scott
Sing Down the Moon

Robbins, Ken
Thunder on the Plains: The Story of the American Buffalo

Rockwell, Thomas
How to Eat Fried Worms

Scieszka, Jon
Knights of the Kitchen Table

Silverstein, Shel
Where the Sidewalk Ends

St. George, Judith
Sacagawea

Independence Day

Read the passage. Then, answer the questions.

The Fourth of July is an important holiday for the United States. It is Independence Day. On July 4, 1776, the United States **declared** that it was a country. It would no longer be part of England. *Independence* means taking care of oneself without relying on help from others. That is why July 4 is called Independence Day. Every Fourth of July, people in the United States celebrate the anniversary of their nation's independence. They celebrate with parades, speeches, and fireworks. People fly American flags to show they are proud of their country.

1. What is the main idea of the passage?

   A. On the Fourth of July, Americans celebrate the anniversary of the United States' independence.
   B. Parades are common on the Fourth of July.
   C. The Fourth of July is for fireworks.

2. Which of the following best defines the word **declared**?

   A. stated or said
   B. celebrated
   C. set off fireworks

3. What are some ways that people celebrate Independence Day?

   Some of us may by
   _have ___ ___ ___ ___ parades._

   _____

One More Chapter

Read the story. Then, write *T* if a statement is true. Write *F* if a statement is false.

Tristan took off his boots and sat on the couch. He looked out the icy window and smiled at the rounded figure in the yard. Tristan rubbed his hands together. Maria was making hot chocolate in the kitchen. He could hear her stirring the pot.

Maria came into the room and handed Tristan his cup. "Hey, nice job out there!" she said. "That carrot makes a great nose. I hope your dad doesn't mind that we borrowed his scarf."

She smiled when Tristan yawned. Maria asked, "Do you want to read a chapter of your book before you go to bed?"

Tristan moaned, "So soon? Can we read two chapters?"

"Your mom said that you have to be in bed by 8:30 because you have school tomorrow," Maria said. She began to read the book aloud. Tristan listened while he drank his hot chocolate.

1. _____ Maria is Tristan's sister.

2. _____ It is winter.

3. _____ A person is standing in the yard.

4. _____ Tristan has been playing outside.

5. _____ Tristan used the scarf to dress a snowman.

6. _____ Maria is a babysitter.

7. _____ It is Saturday night.

8. _____ Tristan's parents are gone for the evening.

African Cat

Read the passage. Then, answer the questions.

If you see a serval, you might notice her ears first. This African cat is about twice the size of a house cat. But, a serval's ears are huge! A serval also has very long legs. These two features make the serval a great hunter.

When servals hunt, they listen with their huge ears to track prey. Their hearing is so good that they can even hear mice running underground. Servals like to hunt in places with tall grass. Because their legs are so long, they can see over the top of the grass. They can jump so high and so fast that they can even catch birds that fly by. Servals can jump up to 10 feet (3 m) in the air!

1. What is the main idea of the passage?
   A. The serval is built to be a great hunter.
   B. The serval has big ears.
   C. The serval lives in Africa.

2. What are two features that make servals great hunters?

   _____

   _____

3. How do servals use these two features to hunt?

   _____

   _____

   _____

What Is the Question?

Read each answer. Then, write an appropriate question for each answer.

1. Question: _____

   Answer: Cinderella, Sleeping Beauty, and Snow White

2. Question: _____

   Answer: a tent, a sleeping bag, and a cooler full of food

3. Question: _____

   Answer: lettuce, broccoli, celery, and zucchini

4. Question: _____

   Answer: He was the first president of the United States.

5. Question: _____

   Answer: Players score points by kicking a ball into a goal. Only the goalie may pick up the ball during play.

6. Question: _____

   Answer: It is a continent at the South Pole. Penguins live there.

7. Question: _____

   Answer: Heat milk on the stove. Then, add chocolate syrup and marshmallows.

8. Question: _____

   Answer: It is a type of animal with six legs, three body sections, and two antennae.

Nellie Bly

Read the passage. Then, answer the questions.

Nellie Bly was a newspaper reporter. When she read a book by Jules Verne titled *Around the World in Eighty Days*, she thought of a great newspaper story. She would make her own trip and do it in fewer than 80 days.

In 1889, a trip around the world was much more difficult than it is today. Back then, the main modes of travel were trains and ships. Also, women did not travel alone much during that time period.

On November 14, 1889, Bly left New York City on a ship called the *Augusta Victoria*. She only took one small handbag with her. Her only clothes were the ones she was wearing. On the first night, a terrible storm rocked the ship. However, the world was watching, and she could not turn back.

When Bly reached England, she learned that Jules Verne wanted to meet her. Bly was excited to meet the famous author. She traveled to France to meet him, losing two nights of sleep to stay on **schedule**.

Bly reached San Francisco, California, with 12 days left. She got on a train that sped across the country in four days. On January 25, 1890, she returned home to New York City and thousands of cheering fans. Bly had traveled around the world in about 72 days. It was a new world record!

1. Choose another good title for the passage.

   A. Breaking World Records
   B. Meeting Jules Verne
   C. The Race around the World

2. Number the events in the order that they happened.

   _____ Bly left on a steamship called the *Augusta Victoria*.

   _____ Bly reached New York City.

   _____ Bly reached San Francisco.

   _____ Bly read *Around the World in Eighty Days*.

   _____ Bly met author Jules Verne.

3. Which of the following best defines the word **schedule**?

   A. a timed plan
   B. a railroad track
   C. a list of things to do

4. What did Bly take with her on her trip?

   _____

   _____

5. Why was traveling around the world difficult for Bly?

   _____

   _____

   _____

Rock Hounds

Read the story. Then, answer the questions.

One afternoon, Anna discovered an interesting rock on the ground in her backyard. She picked it up and examined it closely. Anna took it inside to show her father.

Anna's father looked at the stone and explained that he once had a rock like this in a collection. She asked her father to tell her about his rock collection.

"I had a collection of about 30 rocks," he replied. "I was a rock hound back then," Anna's father laughed.

"You were a what?" Anna asked.

"A rock hound. It is a person who collects rocks," her father said.

"I think I would like to collect rocks as a hobby," Anna said. "It seems interesting. I want to find out where rocks come from and how they are made."

"Rocks are formed by processes in the earth. Some are results of high temperatures. Others are products of immense pressure in the earth. Some rocks are collections of layers of materials," her father explained.

"I think I will start my rock collection right now," Anna said. "Do you want to come with me, Dad?"

"Absolutely!" her dad replied.

1. What is the nickname for a rock collector?

   _____

2. Number the events in the order that they happened.

   _____ Anna showed the rock to her father.

   _____ Anna learned that rock collectors are sometimes called *rock hounds*.

   _____ Anna and her father decided to look for rocks.

   _____ Anna found an interesting rock and picked it up.

   _____ Anna's father explained how rocks are formed.

3. Where did Anna discover an interesting rock?

   A. the neighborhood
   B. the playground
   C. her backyard

4. Imagine that you are starting a rock collection. List five steps to follow to make a rock collection of your own.

   _____

   _____

   _____

   _____

   _____

   _____

   _____

   _____

Recycling

Read the passage. Then, answer the questions.

Garbage trucks pick up trash and take it to dumps. Over time, the piles of trash at the dumps get bigger. The dumps are getting full. Now, we know that some things people throw away can be reused. Recycling trucks come to many homes to pick up these **recyclables**.

Some people sort their recyclables into two separate bins. This is called *two-stream recycling*. One bin holds paper products, and one bin holds plastic, glass, and metal materials. Other people use *single-stream recycling*. They do not sort their recyclables into separate bins.

The recycling trucks collect the recyclables that people leave at their curbs and deliver the materials to recycling centers. In some places, workers sort the materials by hand. But, many places use workers as well as machines to sort the recyclables.

New technology has made recycling centers more **efficient**. Large machines with magnets sort metal materials. The magnets separate steel cans from aluminum cans. The cans are crushed and sent to companies that reuse the metal. Other machines crush paper and cardboard and tie them into bundles. Paper companies buy these bundles to make fresh paper and cardboard.

Recycling is good for many reasons. If we recycle everything we can, garbage dumps will not fill up so quickly. Also, by recycling old materials, we will use fewer new materials. Recycling uses less energy than making new products. Recycling saves fossil fuels and reduces pollution. This is good for our planet's health.

1. What are **recyclables**?

    A. things that can be reused

    B. trash

    C. things that no one wants

2. What does the word **efficient** mean?

    A. slow

    B. productive and without waste

    C. confused

3. Which items belong in each bin? Write the letter of the correct bin next to each item.

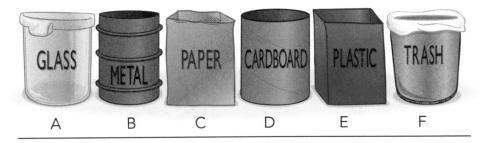

GLASS   METAL   PAPER   CARDBOARD   PLASTIC   TRASH

A   B   C   D   E   F

_____ soup can   _____ used facial tissue

_____ envelope   _____ shampoo bottle

_____ jelly jar   _____ newspaper

_____ junk mail   _____ cereal box

_____ milk jug   _____ yogurt container

_____ soft drink can   _____ broken plate

A Bowl of Blueberries

Read the poem. Then, answer the questions.

A Bowl of Blueberries
by Elizabeth Flikkema

The striped cat
Hovered jealously
Over my bowl of blueberries.
His front legs curled up
Beneath the lip of the bowl.
His nose pressed against
The strange new toys.
Each time I took a **rotund** berry,
He jerked his head up
To watch me slip it
Into my mouth.
He also caught the
Gentle **jostling**
Of the remaining berries
As he stuffed his nose
Back in my bowl of
Ripe,
Dusty blue
Berries
That slipped and sloshed
In that wet, yellow bowl.

1. Has the cat ever seen blueberries before? How can you tell?

   _____

   _____

2. Which word best describes the cat's character?

   A. angry

   B. bored

   C. curious

3. What does the word **rotund** mean in the poem?

   A. flat

   B. skinny

   C. plump

4. What does the word **jostling** mean in the poem?

   A. shaking

   B. squishing

   C. freezing

5. How does the author feel about the cat? How can you tell?

   _____

   _____

   _____

   _____

Animal Diagram

Use the Venn diagram to answer the questions.

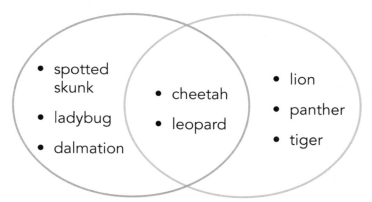

1. What do all of the animals in the left circle have in common (including the area where the circles overlap)?

   _____

2. What do all of the animals in the right circle have in common (including the area where the circles overlap)?

   _____

3. What would be a good title for this diagram?

   _____

4. How would you label each section of the diagram?

   Left Circle: _____

   Right Circle: _____

   Overlap of the Two Circles: _____

Making Money

Read the story. Then, answer the questions.

Jawan wants to go on the class field trip to Washington, D.C., next year. His parents will not just give him the money for the trip. His parents will pay for half of the trip's cost if he earns the other half of the money himself. Jawan has almost a year to earn $150.

Jawan earns some money by mowing lawns. By the end of the summer, Jawan has earned $75. But, he is only halfway to his goal. He earns more money by doing odd jobs for his neighbors.

When autumn arrives, Jawan counts his money. He still needs $40 for his trip. Jawan gets a job delivering newspapers every Sunday. He earns 10¢ for each paper. Every Sunday, he earns $10.

Soon, Jawan has enough money to go on the trip to Washington, D.C. He is just in time. The class trip is on October 21.

Jawan's parents give him the $150 they promised him. Then, Jawan gets his money from his bank and brings all of the money to school. What a great feeling! Jawan has helped pay for his trip.

1. Who is the main character in the story?

   _____

2. What is the problem?

   _____

3. What is the solution to the problem?

   _____

Read the flyer. Then, answer the questions.

Soccer Sign-Ups!

Come to the Pineville Recreation Center to sign up on Saturday, August 6, from 10:00 A.M. to 3:00 P.M. or Wednesday, August 10, from 6:00 P.M. to 9:00 P.M.

The following team categories are available:

Ages 5–7: Boys and Girls Mixed

Ages 8–10: Boys I   Ages 8–10: Girls I

Ages 11–13: Boys II   Ages 11–13: Girls II

Ages 14–16: Boys III   Ages 14–16: Girls III

The fee is $50 per child. The fee includes uniform shirt and shorts. Parents must fill out the forms at registration. Please bring information about your child's medical history, medications, and doctors.

Practices will start after September 1 on weekday afternoons. All games will be played on Saturdays. The season ends November 15.

Call Scott Shaw (soccer **registrar**)
for more information at 555-1234.

We still need volunteer coaches!
Call Kim Chu at 555-2345 if you are interested.

1. On which two dates can you register for soccer?

   _____

   _____

2. How old does a child have to be to register to play soccer?

   _____

3. What is the main purpose of the flyer?

   A.   to explain what a great sport soccer is
   B.   to tell you all you need to know about the soccer season
   C.   to tell you when and how to sign up for soccer

4. Which of the following best defines the word **registrar**?

   A.   a person in charge of registration
   B.   a person who collects money
   C.   a person who works for the recreation department

5. Why do you think the person who made the flyer used large, bold letters at the top?

   A.   to get people's attention
   B.   because they fit at the top
   C.   because the large, bold letters look pretty

The First Man in Space

Read the passage. Then, answer the questions.

In 1957, the former Soviet Union became the first country to send a satellite into space. It was called *Sputnik 1*. At the time, Yuri Gagarin (yur-e gu-gare-in) was a jet pilot in the Russian Air Force. He soon learned that his government wanted to send a human into space. Gagarin wanted that person to be him.

Gagarin was chosen for the cosmonaut training program. Cosmonaut is the Russian word for astronaut. After he was chosen, Gagarin had long days of training and testing. Soon, Gagarin proved that he was ready.

On April 12, 1961, Gagarin climbed inside the tiny capsule of the *Vostok 1* rocket. He wore a heavy spacesuit with boots, gloves, and a white helmet. He waited for the order. Finally, it was time for liftoff.

The rocket roared as it took off into the sky. It left behind a trail of smoke. Inside the capsule, Gagarin was pushed back into his seat. Within minutes, he saw the sky color change from blue to black. Suddenly, he was floating in space.

Gagarin was about 200 miles (322 km) above Earth. He saw a view that no one had seen before. The world looked small and beautiful. He orbited the Earth for 108 minutes.

Then, it was time to go home. The capsule fell back to Earth. A parachute opened to bring Gagarin safely to the ground. He was a hero to his people. His bravery had opened up a new frontier.

1. Number the events in the order that they happened in the passage.

_____ The sky changed from blue to black.

_____ Gagarin was a jet pilot.

_____ A parachute opened to bring Gagarin safely to the ground.

_____ The Soviet Union sent *Sputnik 1* into space.

_____ Gagarin prepared for liftoff.

_____ Gagarin was pushed into his seat as the engines roared.

_____ Gagarin trained to become a cosmonaut.

_____ Suddenly, Gagarin was floating in space.

2. Why do you think that Gagarin was a hero to his people?

_____

_____

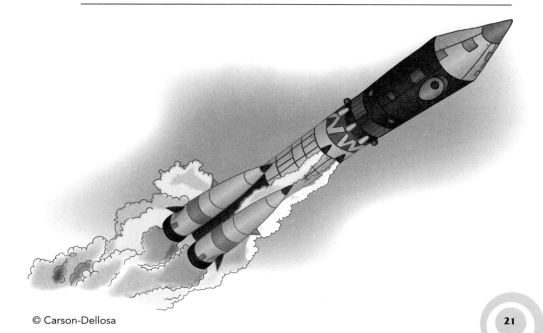

Title, Please!

Read each paragraph. Then, write a title on the line that uses the main idea.

1. _____

Julia's dad called her and her friend Iman over to the boat dock. He had the paddleboat ready for them and held two life jackets in his hands. Julia ran to the boat, put on her life jacket, and sat down. She smiled and waited for Iman. Iman was very nervous. Julia's dad helped Iman put on her life jacket. Iman carefully climbed into the seat and put her feet on the pedals. Julia started pedaling, so Iman did too. Soon they were moving quickly across the water. It was fun! When they were far out in the lake, Julia stopped the boat and said, "Last one in the lake has stinky feet!" Julia jumped in the water. Iman did not move. She did not dare tell Julia that she could not swim. Would Julia laugh at her?

2. _____

We started on the trail early in the morning. The sun was rising in the sky, and the air around us was cold and misty. The pine trees looked like arrows pointing our way to the top of the mountain. My mom and dad each carried a heavy backpack full of food, tents, water, and other things. Ben and I carried backpacks too. Mine only had my clothes and sleeping bag in it. I carried a few snacks in my pockets and two water bottles on my belt. Ben is bigger than I am, so he carried some food and a cookstove in his backpack. We walked quietly at first. I could hear birds singing and chipmunks moving through the leaves on the ground. The air was still, so the trees were silent. We walked single file along the trail.

Lemonade Stand

Read the story. Then, answer the questions.

Felicia and Emily set up a small wooden table at the corner of Cambridge and Sherman streets. Felicia wiped the table and laid out some art supplies. Emily unfolded two chairs and opened a large umbrella to shade the table and chairs.

The girls painted a sign that read, "Lemonade for Sale." They leaned the sign against the table.

Then, Felicia and Emily took the paint inside and came back with a heavy cooler. Inside the cooler were two pitchers of ice-cold lemonade and a bag of ice. The girls also had a container of homemade cookies and some plastic cups.

They took one pitcher out of the cooler and set it on the table. Then, they put 10 cookies on a plate and covered them with plastic wrap. Finally, they sat in their chairs and waited.

Two cars drove by without stopping. A third car came by and parked at the neighbor's house. Felicia and Emily both shouted, "Lemonade for sale! Twenty-five cents a cup!" Felicia's neighbor got out of the car and waved. She walked over to the lemonade stand.

"Hi, Mrs. Garcia," said Emily. "Would you like some lemonade?"

"Yes, please," said Mrs. Garcia. She gave Emily a quarter while Felicia poured lemonade in a cup. "Are those cookies for sale too?" asked Mrs. Garcia. She bought two cookies and said good-bye.

Emily and Felicia stayed at their lemonade stand for two hours. Many people walked by and bought lemonade and cookies. By the time the second pitcher was empty, they had earned six dollars.

1. Number the events in the order that they happened.

_____ Felicia and Emily carried out the heavy cooler.

_____ Emily unfolded the chairs.

_____ Mrs. Garcia bought some lemonade and cookies.

_____ The girls set up the table.

_____ They put 10 cookies on a plate.

_____ They put one pitcher of lemonade on the table.

_____ The girls stayed at the lemonade stand for two hours.

_____ Emily and Felicia earned six dollars.

_____ The girls painted a sign.

_____ Two cars drove by without stopping.

2. If the girls were selling the cookies and the lemonade for 25¢ each, how many did they sell in all? _____

The Midnight Ride

Read the passage. Then, answer the questions.

It was late at night on April 18, 1775. Paul Revere and the American colonists were ready to fight the British king's army. One group of colonists, who called themselves **minutemen**, would be ready to fight at a minute's notice.

First, Revere would wait for a signal from spies who were sent to watch for the arrival of the British army. The minutemen knew that the British army would leave Boston, Massachusetts, and move toward Lexington and Concord. But, they did not know if the army would travel by land or water. Revere was to send a signal to the other minutemen to tell them how the British army would arrive. Next, he would ride quickly toward Lexington to warn the minutemen that the British were coming.

Word came from the spies. Revere called for the signal, which was to hang two lanterns in the Old North Church tower. This meant that the British army was coming by boat. Revere took a boat across the Charles River. He got on a horse and rode into the night.

Paul Revere had to warn the minutemen to prepare for battle. The British army had more men, so the minutemen would have to surprise them. Revere rode through Lexington and warned people. As he rode out of town with two other riders, the British caught him. The other riders managed to escape. One of them made it to Concord to tell the minutemen to be ready.

The British army reached Concord. They had no idea that the minutemen were waiting. The minutemen won their first battle. Someday soon, there would be freedom.

1. Why did some of the colonists call themselves **minutemen**?

_____

_____

_____

2. Number the events in the order that they happened.

_____ British soldiers captured Paul Revere.

_____ Two lanterns hung in the church tower as a signal.

_____ Paul Revere rode through Lexington.

_____ The minutemen surprised the British army in Concord.

_____ Paul Revere received word from the spies.

_____ Another rider warned the minutemen in Concord.

Wilma Rudolph

Read the passage. Then, answer the questions.

Wilma Rudolph was a small, sickly child. She was ill many times during the first years of her life. Rudolph's mother had to take care of her when she was sick with measles, mumps, chicken pox, pneumonia, and scarlet fever. The Rudolph family was very poor, and they could not afford a doctor.

However, one time they had to pay for a doctor. Rudolph had gotten **polio**. Polio is a disease that can damage legs or arms. Today, people can get shots that protect them from polio. But, Rudolph got the disease in the 1940s, well before the shots were created.

The doctor told Rudolph's parents that she would never walk. The doctor put **braces** on her legs, and she did not like them. She also went to the hospital twice a week. It was very hard work to make her legs strong. But, when she was 11 years old, Rudolph wore the braces for the last time.

So, what did Rudolph want to do after barely being able to walk? She wanted to play sports! She started by playing basketball. Rudolph worked hard and practiced until her coach finally let her play. Then, she was so good at playing basketball that she set a state record.

That was only the beginning! Wilma Rudolph went on to become a great **track** star. She won three gold medals in the 1960 Olympics. She was the first woman to do that. It was a long road from her sickness-filled childhood to Olympic gold.

1. Wilma Rudolph became

    A.   a famous track star.

    B.   a famous baseball player.

    C.   the first woman to fly.

2. What does the word **braces** mean in the passage?

    A.   clasps that hold things together

    B.   suspenders

    C.   metal supports for the body

3. List three words that describe Wilma Rudolph as a child.

    _____

    _____

4. Wilma Rudolph was the first _____
to win three gold medals at the Olympics.

5. What is **track**?

    A.   a sport that features passing a ball

    B.   a game like hockey

    C.   a sport that features running

6. What is **polio**?

    A.   an illness that causes blindness

    B.   an illness that can damage arms and legs

    C.   an illness that causes the lungs to fill with fluid

Fact or Opinion

Read each sentence. Then, write _F_ if a statement is a fact. Write _O_ if a statement is an opinion.

A fact is a detail that is real and can be proven. An opinion is a belief that is personal and cannot be proven.

1. _____ The movie I saw last night was the funniest movie ever made.

2. _____ M is the 13th letter of the alphabet.

3. _____ Most people did not vote for the best candidate.

4. _____ The newspaper reported the election's results.

5. _____ Juan's bike has the greatest decorations.

6. _____ Chocolate ice cream with chocolate sauce is the best dessert.

7. _____ The governor should make the school year shorter.

8. _____ The elevator service in the office building is poor.

9. _____ The fruit of an oak tree is the acorn.

10. _____ Banff National Park is Canada's oldest national park.

11. _____ Missouri's state bird should be the cardinal.

12. _____ The Big Dipper and the Little Dipper are constellations.

13. _____ The airplane was scheduled to take off at 5:10 P.M., but it was delayed because of storms.

14. _____ All fourth graders should like pizza.

15. _____ South is the opposite direction of north.

16. _____ All musicians can play the piano well.

17. _____ A golden retriever is bigger than a golden hamster.

18. _____ Students should be able to chew gum in school.

19. _____ The president of the United States lives in the White House.

20. _____ The sun is a star.

21. _____ Canada is north of South America.

22. _____ All girls should play baseball.

Baking Powder Biscuits

Read the recipe. Then, answer the questions.

Ingredients:
- 2 cups (473 mL) all-purpose flour
- 1 tbsp. (15 mL) baking powder
- ½ tsp. (2.5 mL) salt
- 5 tbsp. (70 g) cold, unsalted butter
- ⅔ cup (158 mL) milk

Wash hands and gather the ingredients and the appropriate cooking utensils. Preheat the oven to 450°F (232°C). Measure the flour, the baking powder, and the salt into a large bowl; mix well. Add the butter and **cut in** with a fork. Add the milk and stir with the fork until soft dough forms.

Place the dough on a lightly floured board and knead the dough about 15 times. Roll the dough into a circle about ½ inch (1.25 cm) thick. Cut out biscuits with a 2-inch (5 cm) biscuit cutter. Press the scraps together, roll out, and cut more biscuits. Place biscuits with their sides touching on an ungreased cookie sheet.

With an adult's help, bake the biscuits 12 to 14 minutes until golden brown. Put a clean kitchen towel on a wire cooling rack. Use a spatula to move the hot biscuits to the towel. Fold the towel loosely over the biscuits. Cool for about five minutes before serving.

1. Number the steps in the order that they happen.

    _____ Measure the flour, the baking powder, and the salt into a large bowl and mix well.

    _____ Place the dough on a floured board and knead it 15 times.

    _____ Preheat the oven to 450°F (232°C).

    _____ Add the milk and stir with a fork until soft dough forms.

    _____ Place biscuits with their sides touching on an ungreased cookie sheet.

    _____ Roll the dough into a circle about ½ inch (1.25 cm) thick and cut out biscuits with a 2-inch (5 cm) biscuit cutter.

    _____ Bake 12 to 14 minutes until golden brown.

    _____ Add the butter and cut it in with a fork.

    _____ Loosely fold a kitchen towel over the biscuits and let stand for about five minutes.

2. What do you think it means to **cut in** the butter? _____

    _____

    _____

    _____

Ella and Penny

Read the story. Then, write *T* if a statement is true. Write *F* if a statement is false.

Ella and Penny walked in the hot sun. Ella was sweating, but she kept walking happily. Penny did not know where they were going, but she would go wherever Ella went. When they arrived, a long line had already formed. Ella and Penny got in line. Ella looked ahead. Ten people were waiting ahead of them. Waiting in line would be very hard.

Penny looked around at the people. She noticed a white dog that looked interesting. She wanted to go see the dog, but Ella grabbed her collar. "No," she said. "Stay here with me."

Ella looked ahead again. Now, only five people were ahead of them in line. Ella looked at the sign. She knew what she wanted. She wiped the sweat off of her forehead. Penny was hot too.

Ella was excited. They were next in line. Penny brushed against Ella's leg as if to push her ahead. Ella scratched Penny's neck. "You are right, girl, it is our turn." Ella stepped up to the cart and said, "I will have a single scoop of chocolate chip, please. May I also have a bowl of water for my friend?"

1. _____ Ella and Penny are both children.

2. _____ Penny is a dog.

3. _____ It is a hot, sunny day.

4. _____ Ella and Penny are walking to school.

5. _____ Ella is sweating because she is nervous.

6. _____ Ella and Penny are at a record store.

7. _____ Ella is buying ice cream.

8. _____ Penny is getting ice cream too.

9. _____ Ella is excited.

Draw a picture of Ella and Penny.

Leif Erikson

Read the passage. Then, answer the questions.

Christopher Columbus may not have been the first European to reach North America as once thought. A Viking named Leif Erikson probably was first. He lived about 500 years before Columbus set sail.

More than 1,000 years ago, Vikings ruled the seas. They were known as warriors, but most were farmers and carpenters. Their ships were wooden and small, each with several oars and one sail.

The Vikings came from Norway, but Erikson's family moved to the island of Greenland. Erikson grew up to be a great sailor like his father, Erik the Red. As a young man, Erikson sailed back to Norway. Then, he decided to return to Greenland.

No one is sure what happened next. Vikings told many stories, but most of them were not written down. Many times several **versions** of the same story were told. Some said that Erikson got lost on his trip home to Greenland and landed on North America. Others said that Erikson met a trader who showed him the way to a new land to the west. He probably landed somewhere near Newfoundland.

Erikson thought North America was a great place for farming. The soil was dark and rich. Fish and animals were plenty. Erikson returned to Greenland hoping to bring others back with him to the place he called *Vinland*.

The Vikings disappeared from North America and Greenland, but their stories survived. Their adventures, such as Erikson's journey to Vinland, have become legends.

1. Choose another good title for the passage.

    A. The Discovery of Vinland

    B. Farming in Greenland

    C. North America

2. What did most Vikings do for work?

    _____

    _____

3. Where in North America was Vinland probably located?

    _____

4. Number the events in the order that they happened.

    _____ Erikson's family moved to Greenland.

    _____ Erikson discovered Vinland.

    _____ The Vikings disappeared from North America.

    _____ Erikson sailed to Norway.

    _____ Erikson wanted to return to Greenland.

5. Which of the following best defines the word **versions**?

    A. opinions

    B. books

    C. different accounts

Compost Pile

Read the passage. Then, answer the questions.

Do you throw away all of your garbage? Not everything you throw away is trash. Some garbage can be recycled. Some garbage can be composted. A compost pile is a pile of leaves, grass, and some kinds of leftover foods. It is kept outside and is used for making compost or fertilizer.

It is easy to make a compost pile. To get started, all you need is a small corner of your yard. Some people keep their compost in wooden boxes without lids. Other people buy special bins that mix the compost for them. Things you can put in a compost pile include shredded newspaper, grass, and leaves. You can also put apple peelings, eggshells, and vegetable ends in your compost pile.

It is important to take care of your compost pile. If you do not stir it, it can smell bad. If you take care of your compost, the pile will not get bigger even if you keep adding things to it.

A compost pile can work in two different ways: the sunshine and water help the leaves, grass, and food leftovers rot, or little red worms eat the garbage. In worm composting, worms eat the compost materials, and their bodies turn the food into rich soil.

Having a compost pile is good for many reasons. People who have them throw away less garbage. That means landfills will fill up more slowly. A compost pile can make good fertilizer for your yard, garden, or houseplants. It can be an interesting science experiment too. You will be amazed by how quickly the pile of material gets smaller and by how many animals will make a home there.

1. What is the main idea of the first paragraph?

   A. You should throw away garbage.
   B. A compost pile is kept outside.
   C. Not everything you throw away is trash.

2. What is the main idea of the second paragraph?

   A. A compost pile is simple to make.
   B. You have to buy a special bin.
   C. You make the compost in your yard.

3. What is the main idea of the third paragraph?

   A. Compost is a great fertilizer.
   B. Compost can stink.
   C. You have to take care of your compost pile.

4. What is the main idea of the fifth paragraph?

   A. Animals love compost.
   B. A compost pile is a good thing.
   C. A compost pile is not expensive.

5. Write one supporting detail from each paragraph.

   _____

   _____

   _____

   _____

   _____

How Do Earthquakes Happen?

Read the passage. Then, answer the questions.

Earth has four layers. At Earth's center is the core. The core has two parts: the **inner core** and the **outer core**. The inner core is solid, and the outer core is liquid. The **mantle** surrounds the core. This layer is hot, semisolid rock. The **crust** covers the mantle. As the mantle moves around on the fluid of the outer core, it cracks the crust. The area of crust that breaks is known as a fault.

The cracked crust results in pieces of crust called *plates*. A plate is a large section of Earth's crust. Earth's crust is made up of large and small plates. The plates are continually moving. Sometimes they bump, crunch, or move apart from each other. This movement eventually causes an earthquake.

In an earthquake, the ground moves back and forth and up and down. This movement may last a few seconds or a few minutes. When the shaking occurs, tall buildings can sway, pictures may fall off of walls, and dishes may rattle. Fires may break out if the shaking causes underground gas lines to break. Earthquakes can cause a lot of damage.

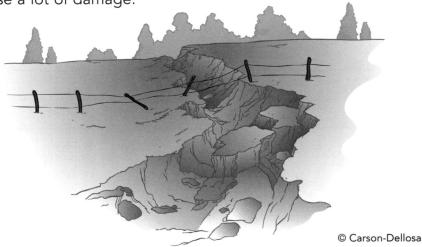

1. Label the layers of Earth on the diagram.

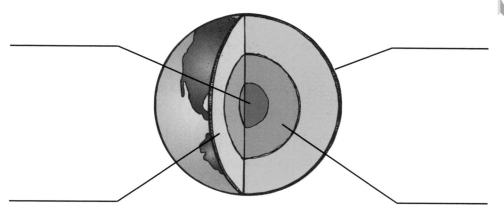

2. What is a crack in Earth's crust called?

_____

3. Why might fires occur during earthquakes?

_____

_____

4. What causes an earthquake?

_____

_____

5. What kinds of damage can an earthquake do?

_____

_____

_____

_____

Maria Mitchell

Read the passage. Then, answer the questions.

Maria Mitchell was born in 1818 during a time when many people thought that women did not need to learn. But, Mitchell's father thought that both boys and girls should go to school. So, he tutored her at home as well as sent her to school.

By the time she was 12 years old, Mitchell was her father's assistant as he studied the stars. As an adult, Mitchell took a job at the library near her Massachusetts home. At night, she and her father used his telescope to look at the sky.

In October 1847, Mitchell saw a bright star through the telescope. She was sure that she had never seen that star before. She carefully wrote notes about the star. The next night, it looked as if the "star" had moved. It also seemed to have a tail! Now, Mitchell was sure that she had found a comet, not a star.

At that time, the king of Denmark was offering a prize to the first person to find a comet that could only be seen through a telescope. Mitchell won the prize! It was a gold medal. But, she won something else too. She won people's respect when they saw that she was serious about her work. Later, the American Academy of Arts and Sciences voted her in as its first female member.

In 1865, a new college just for women opened. It was called Vassar College, and Mitchell became a professor there. She was the first female professor to teach astronomy, or the science of stars and planets. Because of her, female students learned that they could be scientists too. Women could make valuable discoveries to help us understand our world.

1. What is the first paragraph mainly about?

   A. Maria Mitchell's first teaching job
   B. Maria Mitchell's schooling
   C. Maria Mitchell's discovery

2. Who gave Maria Mitchell a gold medal?

   _____

3. Why did receiving the medal win respect for Mitchell?

   A. Before her discovery of the comet, people might not
      have taken a female scientist seriously.
   B. Before she won a medal, Mitchell was not serious
      about her work studying the sky.
   C. Before Mitchell found the comet, nobody thought that
      people would ever see comets through telescopes.

4. What group made Mitchell its first female member?

   _____

5. What was the name of the school where Mitchell taught?

   _____

Shakuntala Devi

Read the passage. Then, answer the questions.

Can you multiply numbers in your head? How about 7,686,369,774,870 times 2,465,099,745,779? That is just one problem that Shakuntala Devi multiplied in her head. And, she finished the problem in only 28 seconds. Devi did not even need a sheet of paper to help her!

This math genius from India was born in 1939. When she was young, the size of a computer was so big that it filled a whole room. Devi could do math problems much faster than those early machines.

Devi was so good at numbers that she went on stage to show her skills. By the time she was eight years old, she had traveled all over India. She could do all kinds of math problems. Devi was especially good at calendar problems. She could instantly figure out the day of the week for any date.

Devi thinks that people use computers too much. She also thinks that students should not use calculators. She thinks that the brain needs exercise like other parts of the body. If Devi had her way, students would not use computers or calculators until they went to college. Until then, their brains would be able to get a real workout!

1. Which of the following information is NOT in the passage?

   A. when Shakuntala Devi was born

   B. where Shakuntala Devi is today

   C. what kinds of math problems Shakuntala Devi can do

2. Devi had traveled all over India by the time she was

   A. three years old.

   B. five years old.

   C. eight years old.

3. What are calendar problems?

   _____

   _____

4. Why does Devi think students should not have computers or calculators until they are in college?

   _____

   _____

Woolly Mammoth

Read the passage. Then, answer the questions.

Finding what is left of **extinct** animals is not new. But, it is always exciting. When scientists find bones, teeth, or horns of an animal, they are happy. When they find more than half of the bones of one animal, it is big news. To find even more is very rare. To find a whole animal with the plants and insects that lived at that time would be impossible. Or would it?

Woolly mammoths are extinct animals that were part of the elephant family. They first walked the earth about 350,000 years ago. Woolly mammoths were most closely related to modern Asian elephants. These big animals had long, thick hair. They lived in cold areas. They also had long, curved tusks, which they used to dig through the snow in search of food.

In 1999, a whole woolly mammoth was found frozen in Siberia. The animal's body had been preserved in ice for more than 20,000 years! Scientists were excited. To be able to study the animal, they had to cut out the giant block of ice. They moved it with a helicopter and took it to an ice cave. To slowly melt the ice, the scientists used hair dryers. It took a long time because they wanted to be very careful.

Scientists are also excited about the plants and insects that were preserved in the ice. By studying them, scientists hope to learn why woolly mammoths no longer exist. Scientists hope to learn many things from this remarkable woolly mammoth.

1. How long ago was it when woolly mammoths first walked on the earth?

   _____

2. What did woolly mammoths use their tusks for?

   _____

3. What did scientists use to melt the ice surrounding the frozen woolly mammoth?

   _____

4. What animal is most closely related to the woolly mammoth?

   _____

5. Number the events in the order that they happened.

   _____ Woolly mammoths became extinct.

   _____ Scientists slowly melted the block of ice so that they could study the woolly mammoth frozen inside.

   _____ A block of ice with a woolly mammoth inside was moved to an ice cave.

   _____ Woolly mammoths first appeared on the earth.

   _____ A frozen woolly mammoth was discovered in 1999.

6. Which of the following best defines the word **extinct**?
   A. no longer existing
   B. old
   C. hard to find

Presidential Facts

Read the advertisement. Then, answer the questions.

Help Wanted:

President of the United States—Must be at least 35 years old and a natural-born citizen of the United States. Must have lived in the United States for at least 14 years. Job lasts for a four-year term but may be extended for one additional term. Current salary is about $400,000 per year plus benefits, including a big white house, a large staff, and a private airplane. Must be willing to relocate to Washington, D.C., and travel frequently. Experience in politics is preferred.

1. A person must be at least _____ years old to run for president of the United States.

   A. 44
   B. 35
   C. 30

2. The job of president lasts for a term of _____ years.

   A. five
   B. eight
   C. four

3. The maximum number of terms a person can serve as president is _____ .

4. The president lives in _____.

   A. Seattle, Washington
   B. Washington, D.C.
   C. Baltimore, Maryland

5. The president earns about _____ per year.

6. A 40-year-old woman who was born in the United States moved to France when she was two years old. She moved back to the United States when she was 30 years old. Can she become the president of the United States? Why or why not?

   _____

   _____

   _____

Finding *Titanic*

Read the passage. Then, answer the questions.

No one thought that the RMS *Titanic* would sink on its first time at sea. But in 1912, the ship hit an iceberg and sank during the night. No one knew exactly where it had sunk. Even if someone had known, it was 12,500 feet (3.8 km) underwater. To search for *Titanic* so deep in the water might be impossible. But, 73 years later, Dr. Robert Ballard thought he had found a way to go that deep.

In 1985, Ballard set out to find the *Titanic*. He would use an unmanned submarine called *Argo*. Ballard's research team steered it by remote control from a ship on the surface. *Argo* had video cameras and lights on it. This let Ballard see the ocean floor.

Argo searched for signs of *Titanic*. For many days and nights, Ballard and his crew found nothing but sand and sea life. Time was running out. Ballard had only four days left before he had to return his boat. He knew this would be his only chance.

Then, Ballard was awakened by one of his men. It was just after one o'clock in the morning. He rushed to the control room. On a screen was the view of one of *Titanic*'s boilers. They had found it!

Argo took amazing pictures of the wreck. Ballard and his crew found that the huge ship was in pieces. The **debris** was spread across one square mile (2.6 km²) of ocean floor. They saw teacups, bottles, shoes, and other belongings of the passengers and crew.

During his career, Ballard has made more than 100 trips underwater. He has done much to teach children about the oceans. But, he will always be thought of as the man who found *Titanic*.

1. Choose another good title for the passage.

   A. The Sinking of *Titanic*
   B. *Argo*
   C. The Man Who Found *Titanic*

2. Why did one of Ballard's men wake him during the night?

   _____

   _____

3. Why did *Titanic* sink?

   _____

   _____

4. Number the events in the order that they happened.

   _____ Ballard rushed to the control room.

   _____ *Titanic* sank.

   _____ Ballard saw nothing but sand and sea life.

   _____ They saw that *Titanic* was in many pieces.

   _____ Ballard used *Argo* to explore the ocean floor.

5. What does the word **debris** mean in the passage?

   A. rocks and sand
   B. the front of a ship
   C. pieces from something broken or destroyed

Cause and Effect

Underline the cause in each sentence. Then, circle the effect.

A **cause** is something that brings a result. That result is called the **effect**.

Example: <u>When it is hot outside,</u> (I sweat a lot.)

1. The heat of the sun evaporates water from lakes and streams.

2. Air currents lift the water vapor into the atmosphere.

3. The water vapor condenses as the rising air cools.

4. Clouds form, and rain may come when too much water vapor is in the air.

5. When water vapor condenses, it may fall in some form of precipitation.

6. Cold air cannot hold much water vapor, so it changes into tiny drops of water called *dew*.

7. Wet clothes hanging on a line dry when all of the water in them evaporates.

8. Water on the ground dissolves nutrients in the soil.

9. A plant gets nourishment when water travels up its stem.

10. Moving water in a river erodes the land.

11. Water expands when it freezes.

12. When the outside air temperature is below 32°F (0°C) for a long period of time, ice forms on ponds.

13. Ice floats on water because it is less dense, or lighter, than water.

14. When salt is thrown on icy sidewalks, the ice melts.

15. Hydroelectric plants convert the energy of flowing water into electricity.

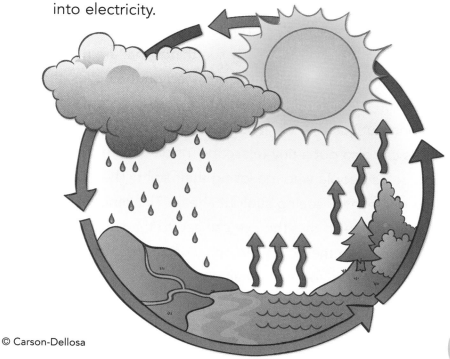

A New Vision

Read the passage. Then, answer the questions.

You may have seen movies in which humans or robots have special **mechanical** eyes. Sometimes they help the hero see farther or better. Could eyes such as these be available in real life? Could a type of camera or telescope help people see? The answer is yes, because cameras and telescopes have lenses just like eyes do.

The lens in the eye helps focus light. The lens curves as the eye looks at things that are nearby. It flattens as the eye looks at things that are far away. A camera lens changes too. In both cases, this change helps keep things from looking blurry. The lens can stop working in a human eye. As people get older, it is harder for their eye lenses to change shape. This makes it harder for those people to see.

Doctors worked to make new lenses for eyes. The lenses are like the lenses in a camera. The doctors can place the lens over the pupil, or black center, of an eye. The lens is held down with hinges. This lens helps people who can only see things that are nearby, not far away. But, after the new lenses are placed on their eyes, these people can see things better far away too. That is because the lens zooms in and out, just like the lens on a camera.

Doctors can also put a tiny telescope inside an eye. The telescope helps people who are losing their sight. The telescope is put into one eye for seeing straight ahead. The other eye is left without a telescope so that the eye can see to the sides. With amazing devices like these, we can only imagine what other ideas might be in the future for the human eye.

1. An eye lens helps focus _____.

2. The black center of an eye is called the _____.

3. When an eye looks at something nearby, the lens _____
   _____.

4. Which of the following best defines the word **mechanical**?

   A. works like a mechanic
   B. works with levers or pulleys
   C. works like a machine

5. How does the lens with hinges help people see better?

   A. It zooms in and out like a camera lens.
   B. It sends a message to a computer chip in the brain.
   C. It makes the eye clear again.

6. What can be put into the eye of a person who is losing his sight?

   A. a new camera held in place with hinges
   B. a tiny telescope
   C. a microchip

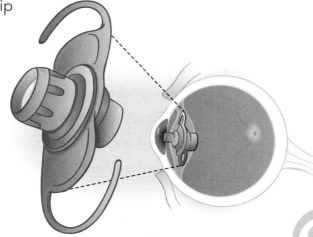

Eunice Shriver

Read the passage. Then, answer the questions.

Eunice Kennedy was born in 1921 in Massachusetts. She grew up in a big family and had eight brothers and sisters. One of her sisters, Rosemary, had difficulties learning. As Kennedy grew up, she knew that she wanted to help other children who were like Rosemary.

After Eunice Kennedy married Robert Sargent Shriver Jr., they lived on a farm in Maryland. Starting in 1962, Eunice Kennedy Shriver held a day camp at the farm every summer. It was for children who had special needs. They could come to the farm and play sports. Shriver always enjoyed playing sports and believed that these children would benefit from doing the same. They played kickball and went swimming. They had fun! Shriver found that many of these children were good at sports just like her sister Rosemary.

Shriver thought that she could take this idea even further. She wanted to hold Olympic games for children and adults with special needs. In 1968, the first Special Olympics were held. One thousand people from 26 U.S. states and Canada took part in the games. The event was held in Chicago, Illinois. It was a big success.

In 1984, Eunice Shriver was awarded the Presidential Medal of Freedom for her amazing work. Today, more than one million athletes around the world take part in the Special Olympics. Games take place in 150 different countries. Even after her death in 2009, Shriver is known for her passion for people with special needs. Her legacy lives on in the Special Olympics.

1. Which word best describes Eunice Shriver's character?

   A. bored
   B. determined
   C. lazy

2. Number the events in the order that they happened.

   _____ Shriver started a camp for children with special needs.

   _____ Shriver got married and moved to a big farm.

   _____ Shriver was awarded the Presidential Medal of Freedom.

   _____ The first Special Olympics event was held.

   _____ Rosemary Kennedy had difficulties learning.

3. Who was Rosemary Kennedy?

   _____

   _____

4. Why did Shriver start a camp at her farm?

   _____

   _____

   _____

5. Where were the first Special Olympics held?

   _____

The Giant Sequoia

Read the passage. Then, answer the questions.

In the California sunshine grows a type of giant tree that has been around for millions of years. The first giant sequoia trees probably started growing more than 200 million years ago and grew throughout North America. Now, these trees only grow naturally in California.

Giant sequoias can live more than 3,000 years. Some giant sequoias can grow as tall as a 25-story building. That is about 250 feet (76 m) tall! Some sequoias have grown as wide as 33 feet (10 m), which is almost as wide as a three-lane highway. But, the biggest giant sequoia living today, called the General Sherman Tree, is 36.5 feet (11.1 m) wide. It is also more than 274 feet (83.5 m) tall.

Not many giant sequoias exist today. Millions of years ago, when giant sequoias grew all over North America, the weather was warmer. At some time, the weather became colder and drier. These trees need warm weather to live. Also, when people visit the remaining giant sequoia forests, they drive and walk all over the ground. This makes the ground hard. The giant sequoias' roots have a hard time soaking water from the hard ground, and this affects their growth.

When a giant sequoia tree dies, it falls onto the forest floor. It continues to help the forest. Many animals build their homes in the fallen tree. As it decays, it becomes fertilizer for other plants. The cycle of life in the giant sequoia forests is amazing to see.

1. Giant sequoia trees have been growing in North America for _____.

2. How tall is the tallest giant sequoia tree?

   A. under 274 feet (83.5 m)
   B. 274 feet (83.5 m)
   C. more than 274 feet (83.5 m)

3. About how many years can a giant sequoia tree live?

   _____

4. Name two reasons why not as many giant sequoias are living now as in the past.

   _____

   _____

   _____

5. What are two things that giant sequoias need to survive?

   _____

   _____

6. How does a fallen giant sequoia help the forest?

   _____

   _____

   _____

   _____

The Leopard That Went for Help

Read the passage. Then, answer the questions.

Billy Arjan Singh was a wildlife expert in India. Singh took care of big cat **orphans**, such as leopards and tigers. According to Singh, one leopard cub orphan that grew up on his farm was named Harriet. But, she was not a pet. Singh taught Harriet how to live in the wild.

After Singh released Harriet to the forest, he kept track of her for a while. He knew when Harriet went off to have cubs of her own. He thought he would never see her again.

Then, floods came to the river and the forest. Harriet and her two cubs were in danger. Even though she had lived in the wild for years, Harriet remembered the place where she had been safe as a cub. She took one of her cubs in her mouth. Then, Harriet swam across the river to Singh's house, walked into the kitchen, and put her cub on the floor. Harriet went back to get her second cub and brought the cub to Singh's house too. Singh's cook moved out and left the kitchen to the leopards!

Harriet watched the river every day. One day, Harriet swam across the river to see her den. She decided that her den was safe. She took the first cub across the river. But, the current in the river was strong. She had trouble swimming back to the farm.

Harriet knew that she should not swim across with the second cub. Instead, Harriet took her cub in her mouth, walked to Singh's boat, and jumped in. When Singh saw Harriet, he knew that she was asking for a ride across the river. Singh rowed the cats to the forest. Harriet and her cubs were at home in the wild again.

1. Who was Harriet?

   A. Singh's sister
   B. Singh's pet
   C. a leopard

2. What are **orphans**?

   A. people or animals left without parents
   B. leopard cubs
   C. animals that live in the wild

3. Why did Singh take Harriet to the forest and leave her there?

   A. He wanted to get rid of her.
   B. He wanted her to live in the wild where she belonged.
   C. He wanted her to live part of the time in the forest.

4. Write *T* if a statement is true. Write *F* if a statement is false.

   _____ Harriet did not trust Singh anymore after she went to live in the wild.

   _____ A huge forest fire put Harriet and her cubs in danger.

   _____ Harriet brought two cubs to Singh's house.

   _____ Singh lived in the forest.

   _____ Singh raised Harriet like a pet.

Making Oatmeal

Read the chart. Then, answer the questions.

Ingredients:	Number of Servings:			
	1	2	4	6
water	1 cup	2 cups	4 cups	6 cups
oats	½ cup	1 cup	2 cups	3 cups
salt	dash	⅛ tsp.	¼ tsp.	⅜ tsp.
raisins (optional)	2 tbsp.	¼ cup	½ cup	¾ cup

1. Riley is making oatmeal for himself and his sister. How much water does he need?

   _____

2. Five people are in Diandre's family, but his dad does not like oatmeal. How many cups of oats does Diandre need?

   _____

3. Samaria has 2½ cups of oats left in the box. Does she have enough to make oatmeal for herself and her friend?

   _____

   How many cups of raisins should Samaria add to the oatmeal?

   _____

4. Felipe's mom asked him to measure the oats for six servings. How much should Felipe measure?

   _____

5. Ryan is making oatmeal for himself and his friend Rashad. Ryan does not like raisins. How many cups of oats does he need?

   _____

   How many raisins does he need?

   _____

Asian and African Elephants

Read the passage. Then, fill in the chart to compare the two types of elephants. If information is not given in the passage, write *not given*.

Asian elephants and African elephants are similar in many ways. But, they are also different.

Asian elephants are smaller. Asian elephants can be up to 9.8 feet (3 m) tall at the shoulder and weigh as much as 5.5 tons (4,990 kg). Asian elephants have smaller ears than African elephants. Asian elephants also have high foreheads and only one "finger" at the end of their smooth trunks. Their front feet have five nails each, and their hind feet have four nails each. Only some males have tusks, and they are small.

African elephants can be up to 12 feet (4 m) tall at the shoulder and weigh as much as 6 tons (5,443 kg). Their ears are big, and their foreheads are sloped. Their front feet have four nails each. Their hind feet have three nails each. Both male and female African elephants have large tusks and wrinkled skin on their trunks.

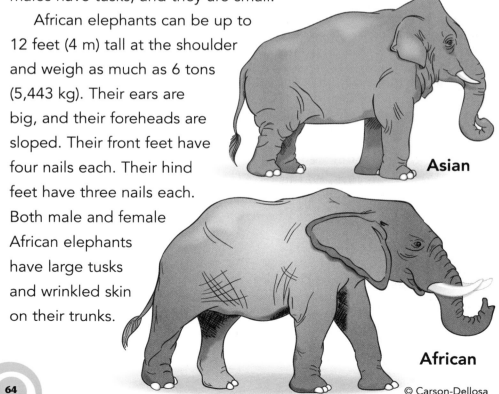

Asian

African

	Asian Elephant	African Elephant
Height:		
Weight:		
Ears:		
Forehead:		
"Fingers" on Trunk:		
Skin on Trunk:		
Nails on Front Feet:		
Nails on Hind Feet:		
Tusks:		

A Solo Flight

Read the passage. Then, answer the questions.

Charles Lindbergh heard about a contest. A prize of $25,000 would go to the first person who could fly an airplane **solo** across the Atlantic Ocean. Many had failed to fly alone to Europe, but Lindbergh knew he could do it.

On the morning of May 20, 1927, Lindbergh was ready to fly from Long Island, New York, to Paris, France. He started his new airplane, *Spirit of St. Louis*, down a muddy runway. As it slowly lifted into the air, the airplane barely missed a telephone line. Leaving behind a cheering crowd, he was now all alone and on his way.

His biggest problem was staying awake. Four hours into the flight, he started to get tired. He flew 10 feet (3 m) above the waves to make himself pay better attention to what he was doing. When that did not work, he opened the windows to feel the cold ocean air.

The next morning, Lindbergh spotted Ireland. By the time he flew over England, he was awake and excited. He turned south toward Paris. He circled the Eiffel Tower and landed his airplane at the nearby airport. He had been alone in the air for 33.5 hours. As he got out of his airplane, hundreds of cheering fans crowded around him. He had won the prize!

When Lindbergh returned home, he was met with a parade, and President Calvin Coolidge gave him several medals. Now, the world was excited about airplanes. Lindbergh had sparked an interest in flying. Someday, this interest would lead to even better airplanes and rockets to the moon.

1. Choose another good title for the passage.

    A.   The First Airplane
    B.   The Long, Lonely Flight
    C.   A Medal from the President

2. What was the name of Lindbergh's airplane?

    _____

3. What was the first thing Lindbergh did to stay awake?

    _____

4. In what city was the airport where Lindbergh landed?

    _____

5. How much time did Lindberg's trip across the ocean take?

    _____

6. Number the events in the order that they happened.

    _____ Lindbergh opened the windows on his airplane.

    _____ Lindbergh's airplane barely missed a telephone line.

    _____ Lindbergh flew around the Eiffel Tower.

    _____ Calvin Coolidge gave Lindbergh a medal.

    _____ Hundreds of cheering fans crowded around Lindbergh.

7. Which of the following best defines the word **solo**?

    A.   without sleep
    B.   without lessons
    C.   done by one person

Idioms

Read each story. Then, circle the best meaning for the bold idiom.

An idiom is an expression that has a unique meaning that cannot be figured out from context clues.

Lee's friends were talking about the baseball World Series. Some of them thought the Dodgers would win. Some of them thought it would be the Yankees. They asked Lee, "Which team do you think will win?"

"They are both great teams," said Lee.

His friends groaned, "**Do not sit on the fence**."

1. A. Do not break the fence.
   B. Choose one side or the other.
   C. Be careful not to fall.

Eboni saved her money for a new game. She helped her mom send in the order. She could hardly wait for the game to come. Every day, Eboni went to the mailbox. Every day, she came back sad. Her package was not there.

Finally, she gave up. She did not check the mail. She went to Alicia's house instead. When she got home, the package was on her bed.

Then, her mother said, "I could have told you that **a watched pot never boils**."

2. A. Things seem to take longer if you check on them a lot.
   B. You should not watch videos.
   C. Water will not boil if you stare at it.

Space Probes

Read the passage. Then, answer the questions.

We learn about planets by observing them. Scientists use telescopes to see planets. A telescope is a tool that makes distant objects look bigger. Some planets are too far away to see clearly, even with a telescope. How do we learn about these planets?

Scientists send devices called **space probes** into space. The probes have telescopes and cameras that record what they see. Space probes also carry tools to gather information about the weather and the soil on other planets. The information is sent back to the earth so that scientists can study it.

Mariner 2 was the first successful space probe. It was launched in 1962. It gave scientists information about the planet Venus. Since then, scientists have sent many more probes into space.

1. What is the main idea of the passage?

   A. Space probes tell us about other planets.
   B. Telescopes help us see other planets.
   C. *Mariner 2* was the first successful space probe.

2. What is a **space probe**?

   _____

   _____

3. What information about other planets can space probes gather?

   _____

   _____

Cars of the Future

Read the passage. Then, complete the Venn diagram.

Will cars of the future run on gas? Many people do not think so. They think that new cars will be invented. These new cars would use different things for fuel. The new fuel would be better for the environment. It would be cheaper than gas. It would make cars run longer for less money.

Some people say that electricity would be a good fuel. We already put electric motors that run on batteries into machines that used to run on gas. We also put electric motors in hybrid cars. But, could cars run only on batteries?

So far, battery-operated cars have not been successful. One problem with batteries is what might happen when the batteries run low. When a car runs out of gas, the driver buys more. But, it takes time to charge a battery. Many people would not want to wait for batteries to charge before they could continue driving.

Fuel cells are another idea for fueling cars. Like batteries, fuel cells create energy with a chemical reaction. Unlike batteries, fuel cells do not need to be recharged. These cells run on liquid hydrogen, which can be changed into a gas. Some fuel cell vehicles, called *FCVs*, have already been tested. Fuel cell vehicles cannot go as fast as gas cars. They also have to be made of lighter metals. But, they can drive about 120 miles (193.2 km) before needing more fuel. And, FCVs do not pollute the air at all.

Scientists have many great ideas for future cars. But, they still have a lot of work to do before people can start driving them.

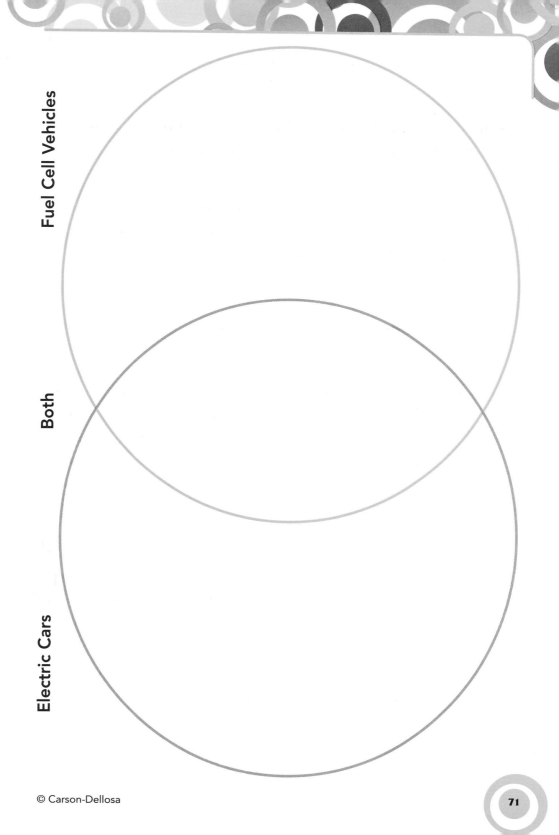

Fuel Cell Vehicles

Both

Electric Cars

Context Clues

Read each story. Then, decide which statement following the story is true. Circle the letter of your choice.

1. Ardon skimmed the surface in his solar pod. He had to make it back to Astra City before the third moon rose. Longa was waiting for him. He had promised that he would not be late.

    A. This story takes place in another country.
    B. This is a true story.
    C. This story takes place on another planet.

2. Julia wished she could go back to her room. She had not chosen to be the daughter of a queen. The line of people waiting to bow before her stretched all the way across the throne room. The crown was heavy, and it made her head itch, but she could not scratch. She had to sit still and smile.

    A. Julia is a horse.
    B. Julia is a princess.
    C. Julia is a chef.

3. Jason hid behind a tree at the edge of the village. He was watching for the messenger. He had been told that the man would come on horseback. The man would not stop. He would throw a bag to Jason and keep going. Jason looked around. He could not let anyone see him.

    A. Jason is taking part in a secret plan.
    B. Jason is studying.
    C. Jason is eating dinner.

Predicting Outcomes

Read each incomplete story. Then, circle the best outcome.

1. Laura had worked in the garden all day. Her back ached, and she felt dirty. After dinner, she _____.

    A.   went to bed.
    B.   took a bath.
    C.   read a book.

2. During a soccer game, the team's star player twisted her ankle. She could not finish the game. The team _____.

    A.   tried to win without her.
    B.   tried to tie the game.
    C.   tried to finish the game.

3. Sam was bored. He had been playing alone all morning. He called his friend John, but John was not at home. Then, the phone rang. It was his friend Jason. Jason asked Sam _____.

    A.   to come over to play.
    B.   what the homework assignment was.
    C.   when the next baseball game was.

4. We let our cat out for his nightly exercise. Unfortunately, the neighbor's dog was outside. The cat ran up a tall tree. He would not come down. We had to _____.

    A.   call for help.
    B.   go to bed.
    C.   sit on the ground and wait.

Letter Sort

Rearrange each set of letters to name something that can be warm, hot, or spicy. Write the letters in the spaces.

1. A D Y __ ◯ __

2. C E E F F O ◯ __ __ __ __ __

3. A E R T W __ __ __ __ __

4. N S U __ __ __

5. A E T ◯ __ __

6. A O O P T T __ ◯ __ __ __ ◯

7. A C E S U __ __ ◯ __ __

8. E E P P P R S __ ◯ __ __ __ __ __

9. A A L S S __ __ ◯ __ __

10. C H I I L __ ◯ __ __ __

Rearrange the circled letters to name something else that can be warm or hot.

__ __ __ __ __ __ __ __ __

Lose the Letters

Look at each word. Make a new word by dropping one letter. Keep the remaining letters in the same order. Continue doing this until a two-letter word is left.

1. stone

— — — —

— — —

— —

2. plane

— — — —

— — —

— —

3. bread

— — — —

— — —

— —

4. grasp

— — — —

— — —

— —

5. print

— — — —

— — —

— —

6. train

— — — —

— — —

— —

Multiple-Meaning Words

Each word below has more than one meaning. Write two sentences for each word. In each sentence, use the word differently.

conduct

1. _____

_____

2. _____

_____

content

3. _____

_____

4. _____

_____

desert

5. _____

_____

6. _____

_____

Applying Analogies

Choose a word from the word bank to complete each analogy. Write the word on the line. Then, circle the answers in the puzzle.

thermometer	money	canoe	ladle
mammal	leather	window	snow

1. Wind is to sailboat as oar is to _____ .
2. Sweater is to wool as boot is to _____ .
3. Weight is to scale as temperature is to _____ .
4. Vase is to flowers as wallet is to _____ .
5. Water is to ice as rain is to _____ .
6. Carpenter is to hammer as cook is to _____ .
7. Scale is to fish as fur is to _____ .
8. Paper is to book as glass is to _____ .

k	r	s	n	o	w	l	d	r	t	l	f
t	h	e	r	m	o	m	e	t	e	r	g
i	b	r	z	n	a	h	c	a	e	k	s
m	m	g	l	s	t	n	w	p	s	e	e
o	a	u	l	a	h	o	c	a	n	o	e
n	c	m	e	v	d	e	h	w	a	x	z
e	n	l	m	n	m	l	o	i	k	w	m
y	f	t	i	a	c	h	e	q	e	f	q
m	y	w	j	d	l	s	y	a	f	o	n

Answer Key

Page 4
1. A.; 2. A.; 3. with parades, speeches, fireworks, flying flags

Page 5
1. F; 2. T; 3. F; 4. T; 5. T; 6. T; 7. F; 8. T

Page 6
1. A.; 2. They have big ears and long legs.; 3. They use their great hearing to track prey. They use their long legs to hunt in tall grass.

Page 7
Answers will vary, but may include:
1. What are the names of three fairy-tale princesses?; 2. What things do you take on a camping trip?; 3. What are four green vegetables?; 4. Who was George Washington?; 5. How do you play soccer?; 6. What is Antarctica?; 7. How do you make hot chocolate?; 8. What is an insect?

Page 9
1. C.; 2. 2, 5, 4, 1, 3; 3. A.; 4. one small handbag; 5. The main modes of travel were trains and ships. Women did not often travel alone.

Page 11
1. a rock hound; 2. 2, 3, 5, 1, 4; 3. C.; 4. Answers will vary.

Page 13
1. A.; 2. B.; 3. soup can–B; envelope–C; jelly jar–A; junk mail–C; milk jug–E; soft drink can–B; used facial tissue–F; shampoo bottle–E; newspaper–C; cereal box–D; yogurt container–E; broken plate–F

Page 15
1. No. They are strange new toys.; 2. C.; 3. C.; 4. A.; 5. The author likes the cat. The cat is allowed to be close to and play with the author's food.

Page 16
1. All of the animals have spots.; 2. All of the animals are in the big cat family.; 3.–4. Answers will vary.

Page 17
1. Jawan; 2. Jawan wants to go on the trip to Washington, D.C., but his parents will not give him all of the money.; 3. Jawan will work to earn half of the money, and his parents will give him the other half.

Page 19
1. August 6 and 10; 2. 5; 3. C.; 4. A.; 5. A.

Page 21
1. 6, 2, 8, 1, 4, 5, 3, 7; 2. Answers will vary.

Pages 22–23
Answers will vary.

Page 25
1. 4, 2, 8, 1, 6, 5, 9, 10, 3, 7; 2. 24

Page 27
1. They called themselves minutemen because they would be ready to fight at a minute's notice.; 2. 4, 2, 3, 6, 1, 5

Page 29
1. A.; 2. C.; 3. Answers will vary but may include: *small, sickly, tough, determined*; 4. woman; 5. C.; 6. B.

Page 30
1. O; 2. F; 3. O; 4. F; 5. O; 6. O; 7. O; 8. O; 9. F; 10. F; 11. O; 12. F; 13. F; 14. O; 15. F; 16. O; 17. F; 18. O; 19. F; 20. F; 21. F; 22. O

Page 33
1. 2, 5, 1, 4, 7, 6, 8, 3, 9; 2. to mix with a chopping motion

Page 35
1. F; 2. T; 3. T; 4. F; 5. F; 6. F; 7. T; 8. F; 9. T

Answer Key

Page 37
1. A.; 2. They were farmers or carpenters.; 3. somewhere near Newfoundland; 4. 1, 4, 5, 2, 3; 5. C.

Page 39
1. C.; 2. A.; 3. C.; 4. B.; 5. Possible details: Some things can be recycled. Some things can be composted.; You can use a box or a special bin. You put in shredded newspaper, grass, and leaves. You can put in some kinds of food garbage.; You have to stir it. You have to allow the sun to reach it. You should water it lightly.; People throw away less garbage. Compost makes good fertilizer. A compost pile is an interesting science experiment.

Page 41
1.

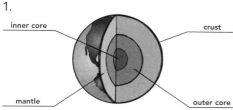

inner core crust

mantle outer core

2. fault; 3. Underground gas lines may break.; 4. Plates bump, crunch, or move apart from each other.; 5. Pictures may fall off of walls, dishes may rattle and break, gas lines may break, and fires may start.

Page 43
1. B.; 2. the king of Denmark; 3. A.; 4. American Academy of Arts and Sciences; 5. Vassar College

Page 45
1. B.; 2. C.; 3. A challenge to instantly figure out the day of the week for any date.; 4. She thinks that the brain needs exercise like other parts of the body.

Page 47
1. 350,000 years ago; 2. They used their tusks to dig through snow to find food.; 3. hair dryers; 4. The modern Asian elephant; 5. 2, 5, 4, 1, 3; 6. A.

Page 49
1. B.; 2. C.; 3. two; 4. B.; 5. $400,000; 6. No, because she has not lived in the United States for at least 14 years.

Page 51
1. C.; 2. They found one of *Titanic's* boilers.; 3. It hit an iceberg.; 4. 4, 1, 3, 5, 2; 5. C.

Pages 52–53
(Students should circle the orange text.)
1. The heat of the sun evaporates water from lakes and streams.;
2. Air currents lift the water vapor into the atmosphere.; 3. The water vapor condenses as the rising air cools.;
4. Clouds form, and rain may come when too much water vapor is in the air.;
5. When water vapor condenses, it may fall in some form of precipitation.;
6. Cold air cannot hold much water vapor, so it changes into tiny drops of water called *dew*.; 7. Wet clothes hanging on a line dry when all of the water in them evaporates.; 8. Water on the ground dissolves nutrients in the soil.; 9. A plant gets nourishment when water travels up its stem.; 10. Moving water in a river erodes the land.;
11. Water expands when it freezes.;
12. When the outside air temperature is below 32°F (0°C) for a long period of time, ice forms on ponds.; 13. Ice floats on water because it is less dense, or lighter, than water.; 14. When salt is thrown on icy sidewalks, the ice melts. 15. Hydroelectric plants convert the energy of flowing water into electricity.

Answer Key

Page 55
1. light; 2. pupil; 3. curves; 4. C.; 5. A.; 6. B.

Page 57
1. B.; 2. 3, 2, 5, 4, 1; 3. She was Eunice Shriver's sister.; 4. She wanted children like Rosemary to have a chance to play sports.; 5. Chicago, Illinois

Page 59
1. more than 200 million years; 2. C.; 3. more than 3,000 years; 4. The weather is not as warm or as wet as it once was. People trample the ground near their roots.; 5. They need water and warmth.; 6. It creates animal homes and fertilizer.

Page 61
1. C.; 2. A.; 3. B.; 4. F, F, T, F, F

Page 63
1. 2 cups; 2. 2 cups; 3. yes, 1/4 cup; 4. 3 cups; 5. 1 cup, 2 tbsp.

Page 65
Asian Elephant: 9.8 feet, 5.5 tons, small, high, 1 finger, smooth, five on front, four on hind; some males—small; **African Elephant**: 12 feet, 6 tons, big, sloped, not given, wrinkled, four on front, three on hind; males and females—large

Page 67
1. B.; 2. *Spirit of St. Louis*; 3. He flew just 10 feet (3 m) above the ocean.; 4. Paris, France; 5. 33.5 hours; 6. 2, 1, 3, 5, 4; 7. C.

Page 68
1. B.; 2. A.

Page 69
1. A.; 2. a spacecraft sent to investigate other planets; 3. weather, type of soil, what it looks like

Page 71
Answers will vary, but may include: Electric Cars: use batteries, take time to recharge; Fuel Cell Vehicles: use liquid hydrogen, can go about 120 miles (193.2 km) before refueling; Both: chemical reactions create power, do not use gas so they are better for the environment

Page 72
1. C.; 2. B.; 3. A.

Page 73
1. B.; 2. A.; 3. A.; 4. A.

Page 74
1. day; 2. coffee; 3. water; 4. sun; 5. tea; 6. potato; 7. sauce; 8. peppers; 9. salsa; 10. chili; mystery word: chocolate

Page 75
1. stone, tone, one/ton, on/to; 2. plane, pane/plan, pan, an; 3. bread, bead/ read, bed/bad/red, be/ad/Ed; 4. grasp, gasp/rasp, gas/asp, as; 5. print, pint, pin/pit, in/it; 6. train, rain, ran, an

Page 76
Answers will vary.

Page 77
1. canoe; 2. leather; 3. thermometer; 4. money; 5. snow; 6. ladle; 7. mammal; 8. window

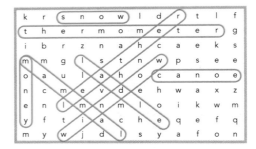